METAMORPHOSIS
POEMS INSPIRED BY TITIAN

METAMORPHOSIS

POEMS INSPIRED BY TITIAN

THE NATIONAL GALLERY COMPANY, LONDON
DISTRIBUTED BY YALE UNIVERSITY PRESS

Published to accompany the exhibition
Metamorphosis: Titian 2012
The National Gallery, London
11 July – 23 September 2012

Sponsored by Credit Suisse

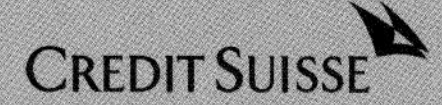

National Gallery publications generate valuable revenue for the Gallery to ensure that future generations are able to enjoy the paintings as we do today.

First published in Great Britain in 2012 by
National Gallery Company Limited
St Vincent House
30 Orange Street
London WC2H 7HH
www.nationalgallery.org.uk

ISBN 978-1-85709-547-0
1034100

British Library Cataloguing-in-Publication Data
A catalogue record is available from the British Library

Editor: Kate Bell
Design: Smith & Gilmour
Picture Research: Suzanne Bosman
Production: Jane Hyne and Penny Le Tissier

Colour reproduction by DL Repro Limited
Printed by Pureprint, England

CONTENTS

PREFACE

To mark the London 2012 Olympics, the National Gallery has collaborated with the Royal Opera House to exhibit a wide range of contemporary British artistic activity. Ballets have been commissioned, with scenery, sets and costumes by three of Britain's foremost artists. All have been inspired by Titian's paintings of *Diana and Callisto*, *Diana and Actaeon* and *The Death of Actaeon*, and by the poetry of Ovid that Titian was illustrating. The ballets will be performed at Covent Garden and their designs will be on display at the National Gallery. In addition, leading contemporary poets have been invited to respond to the same paintings and texts. These poems, published separately here, will also feature in the exhibition.

Both exhibition and publication have been made possible by our partnership with Credit Suisse which has given us the confidence, as well as the means, to undertake this initiative. With it, we hope to demonstrate how both Old Master paintings and ancient literature can generate new music, dance, design and poetry.

It is a great tribute to the National Gallery and to the National Galleries of Scotland (with whom we have aquired two of the three Titians) that the fourteen poets commissioned have responded so positively. It is a tribute also to the expert panel which invited them. I am most grateful to Antonia Byatt who chaired the panel and to Ruth Borthwick, Stephen Gill, Daisy Goodwin, Nicola Normanby, Richard Price and Eric Wagner who agreed to sit on it.

Particular thanks are also due to Jillian Barker, Director of Education, Information and Access, who initiated and managed this undertaking assisted by Sarah Taylor, and to Carol Plazzotta for her help with the introductory essay, which has also been much improved by Mary Crettier.

NICHOLAS PENNY
Director, The National Gallery, London

OVID, TITIAN, AND ENGLISH POETRY

The stories of Diana and Callisto and of Diana and Actaeon were told by the great Latin poet Ovid (Publius Ovidius Naso) in the *Metamorphoses*, a poem in fifteen 'books', written in the first years of the Christian era. In this long poem Ovid wove together into a continuous narrative numerous episodes of mythology known to him from Greek literature. Beginning with the creation of heaven and earth and concluding with more modern heroes as well as the family of Augustus, the ruling emperor, it dwells mostly on the amorous adventures of the gods of Olympus.

Callisto's story is told in the second book (lines 417–95). A favourite nymph of the goddess Diana, she was raped by Jupiter and, when rejected by Diana on account of her pregnancy, was turned into a bear by Jupiter's jealous wife, Juno. The mortal hunter Actaeon, whose tragic encounter with Diana is related in the third book (lines 165–231), was turned into a stag and torn to pieces by his own hounds. Their stories are not linked by Ovid, but the Venetian artist Titian (Tiziano Vecellio; active about 1506; died 1576) made them the subjects of a pair of paintings that he sent to Philip II of Spain in 1559. The works have remained together ever since and in 2012 are shown in London for the first time in more than half a century. Both pictures illustrate the punishment inflicted by the indignant Diana, chaste goddess of the hunt, on an innocent victim – male in one case, female in the other. Most of Ovid's stories involve the idea of transformation, or metamorphosis, and in both of these stories the victims are turned into animals: Actaeon into a stag, Callisto into a bear. There are other tranformations: Jupiter embraces Callisto by taking on the appearance of Diana, and both Callisto and her son Arcas are finally changed into constellations.

It is a striking fact that both Titian and Shakespeare, the painter and the poet who brought the world of ancient mythology and history most vividly to life in the Renaissance, were limited in their knowledge of Latin – perhaps even, in the case of Titian, almost entirely ignorant of it. Of all the ancient poets, Ovid was the best known throughout medieval Europe. Excerpts from his poems were used in teaching, and the episodes in the *Metamorphoses* in particular were also given allegorical interpretations, often naively didactic (as when the story of Actaeon was said to teach how ruinously foolish it could be to keep a pack of hounds), sometimes elaborately fanciful (as when stories were paralleled with episodes in the Old Testament). For his paintings Titian depended on a recent Italian translation by Giovanni Andrea dell'Anguillara (1554), one of the first to capture something of Ovid's original magic. Titian may also have consulted the translation published in 1553 by his friend and champion the humanist Lodovico Dolce. And Callisto's tale is recounted more briefly in Ovid's *Fasti*, which he had consulted when painting mythological scenes for Alfonso d'Este almost forty years earlier.

In Britain the first published translation of the *Metamorphoses*, that by Arthur Golding, began to appear in print in 1565 and was completed in 1567. Another version was made by George Sandys in 1626 and reprinted with a commentary in 1632. The finest translations – the work of John Dryden, Joseph Addison and Alexander Pope, among others – were gathered into a highly popular anthology by Sir Samuel Garth in 1717. The elegance, precision and wit embodied in the antithetical structure of the heroic couplet, then favoured by English poets, owed much to the example of Latin poetry and of Ovid in particular.

Then, suddenly, in the late eighteenth century Ovid fell from high esteem. He was still read, but both Wordsworth and Goethe record the disapproval that met their early enthusiasm for his

Eugène Delacroix (1798–1863)
Ovid among the Scythians, 1859
Oil on canvas, 87.6 x 130.2 cm
The National Gallery, London, NG 6262

poetry. The new interest in early Greek civilisation developed at the expense of admiration for the Hellenistic and the Roman epochs. The myths as retold by Ovid now began to seem like mere elegant entertainments devised for sophisticated metropolitan society, far removed from the terrors of the forest, the horror of the unclean, the idea of magical possession and the force of elementary passions. For those who were fascinated by the contrast between primitive and decadent societies, however, Ovid himself became a subject. Before the *Metamorphoses* had been completed, he was expelled from Rome, by order of the emperor, for an offence which is unknown to us, and forced to dwell on the eastern fringes of the Empire, among the wild Scythians. Eugène Delacroix, in particular, was captivated by the romantic story of Ovid's exile, and first treated this subject among the ceiling decorations of the library of the Palais Bourbon in Paris in 1844. A dream-like version that he exhibited at the Paris Salon in 1859, in which the Scythians are shown milking a wild mare and delivering drink to the Roman poet in a pail, is today in the National Gallery.

Modern translators, most notably Ted Hughes, seem often to dwell on the raw original myth and the natural violence that lies below Ovid's often mellifluous and elegant verse.

> Every hound filled its jaws
> Till there was hardly a mouth not gagged and crammed
> With hair and muscle. Then began the tugging and the ripping.

Gag, cram, tug and rip are Anglo-Saxon verbs. It is a strength of the English language that it has two strata with low, blunt, rude and primitive words lurking below elevated, ceremonial, academic and poetic diction. Paradoxically, the latter (to which Hughes is averse) is Latinate and much of it imported into English by those who hoped to emulate the original language of Ovid and other great Roman writers.

As for Titian, although he was in some respects further removed than Ovid from the world which gave birth to these myths, in other respects he was closer. Majesty, for a Venetian in the sixteenth century, required more than natural accessories and environment. He weaves strings of pearls in Diana's hair and provides her with an elegant fountain and grotto to bathe in. In one of the paintings he gives her a lapdog such as accompanied every great lady in the Italy of his day. His paintings include passages which are lyrical and comic as well as tragic, matching Ovid's poetry in their variety. And, yet, certain values fundamental to these myths – those of virginity and of vendetta, for example – were cherished in the society in which he worked, far more than among educated Western Europeans today and perhaps more so than among the Roman public for which Ovid wrote.

Titian referred to his large-scale mythologies as *poesie*, for he believed they were equivalent to poetry not subordinate to it. In doing so he was probably advised, and was certainly sanctioned, by the great writers who were his close friends (most notably Pietro Aretino, but also Dolce). They were not Titian's first paintings of this kind. Amorous episodes from mythology, usually taken from Ovid, had become popular for the decoration of furniture made for newlyweds, and there are some examples of this among Titian's earliest surviving paintings.

When Titian was commissioned in 1518 to paint three subjects from pagan mythology for a special room in the palace of the duke of Ferrara, something more ambitious was required. It is likely that he was supplied with literary sources by the duke's advisers, and in the third and last of these paintings, which we take to be *Bacchus and Ariadne*, he seems to have been entrusted to combine two different sources, the *Carmina* by Catullus and Ovid's *Ars Amatoria*. *Bacchus and Ariadne* is, arguably, the first poetic narrative by the artist that truly foreshadows the *poesie*

Titian (active about 1506; died 1576)
Bacchus and Ariadne, 1520–3
Oil on canvas, 176.5 x 191 cm
The National Gallery, London, NG 35

he invented, first for the Farnese (the family of Pope Paul III), and later for Philip II, king of Spain, the most powerful monarch in Europe. In other words, this painting, one of the most famous in the National Gallery, is the first step towards the paintings of Diana, which are now also to be seen there and in the Scottish National Gallery.

The story of Callisto begins with Jupiter 'the omnipotent' reviewing the damage caused to the world, and in particular to his beloved Arcadia, by Apollo's son, Phaeton, who has scorched the earth in an unsuccessful attempt to drive his father's chariot. While repairing the woods and streams he spies Callisto who, it is explained, was not one of those homely types who spend their time spinning wool nor one of those vain creatures who devote themselves to dressing their hair, but a sporting girl, loosely dressed, with flying locks. Although a favourite of the goddess Diana, on this morning she has been hunting alone:

> The sun now shone in all its strength, and drove
> The heated virgin panting to a grove;
> The grove around a grateful shadow cast:
> She dropt her arrows, and her bow unbrac'd;
> She flung herself on the cool grassy bed;
> And on the painted quiver rais'd her head,
> Jove saw the charming huntress unprepar'd,
> Stretch'd on the verdant turf, without a guard.
> 'Here I am safe,' he cries, 'from Juno's eye;
> Or shou'd my jealous queen the theft descry,
> Yet wou'd I venture on a theft like this,
> And stand her rage for such, for such a bliss!'
> Diana's shape and habit strait he took,
> Soften'd his brows, and smooth'd his awful look,
> And mildly in a female accent spoke.
> 'How fares my girl? How went the morning chase?'
> To whom the virgin, starting from the grass,

'All hail, bright deity, whom I prefer
To Jove himself, tho' Jove himself were here.'
The God was nearer than she thought, and heard
Well-pleas'd himself before himself preferr'd.

ADDISON

Jupiter (Jove) embraces her but as she attempts to relate the detail of her morning's activities he stops her mouth with eager kisses, and his actions then

Bewrayèd plainly what he was and wherefore that he came.
The wench against him strove as much as any woman could.
I would that Juno had it seen, for then I know thou would
Not take the deed so heinously. With all her might she strove.
But what poor wench or who alive could vanquish mighty Jove?

GOLDING

Callisto is left so confused and fearful that, when she sees the real Diana, she trembles at the prospect of further deceit but, on seeing her companion nymphs, she joins them. They sense that something has happened to her. Months pass and one day, hot from the hunt, Diana spies a clear stream concealed by trees and urges her nymphs to bathe there:

Only the blushing huntress stood confus'd,
And form'd delays, and her delays excus'd;
In vain excus'd: her fellows round her press'd,
And the reluctant nymph by force undress'd,
The naked huntress all her shame reveal'd,
In vain her hands the pregnant womb conceal'd;
'Begone!' the Goddess cries with stern disdain,
'Begone! nor dare the hallow'd stream to stain':
She fled, for ever banish'd from the train.

ADDISON

This is the moment – and the words – which Titian chose to depict. The expressions on the faces, and the matching 'body language', are among the most remarkable in any of his paintings. The status of Callisto as favourite of the goddess has been emphasised earlier in the poem. Now the envy of her companions finds an outlet in a new sort of blood sport. The character of the sky and the woods, and the broken stream of water that falls from the fountain, quivering in sympathy, hint at the tragic outcome.

Diana's indignation is swiftly followed by Juno's revenge. As soon as the child, Arcas, is born, Juno descends to earth, takes hold of Callisto and pulls her along the ground. As she is being dragged she begins to grow hairy and her nails turn into claws, for Juno has transformed her into a bear – a bear with the mind of a human being but unable to speak, a bear that fears its own kind as well as other wild creatures. Fifteen years pass, during which Callisto's son grows up to be a keen huntsman.

> Upon his mother suddenly it was his chance to light;
> Who for desire to see her son did stay herself from flight
> And wistly on him cast her look, as one that did him know.
>
> GOLDING

Arcas overcomes his fright and raises his javelin to slay her,

> But God Almighty held his hand and, lifting both away,
> Did disappoint the wicked act. For straight he did convey
> Them through the air with whirling winds to top of all the sky
> And there did make them neighbour stars about the pole on high.
>
> GOLDING

Juno, infuriated by this unexpected outcome, rushes to the gods of the ocean to implore them not to permit these new stars to bathe in the sea.

The story of Diana and Actaeon opens with Actaeon and his companions hunting on a mountainside, the ground of which is stained with the blood of numerous beasts. Actaeon bids his men to rest because of the heat. He does not know how near he is to another hunting party.

Down in a vale with pine and cypress clad,
Refresh'd with gentle winds, and brown with shade,
The chaste Diana's private haunt, there stood
Full in the centre of the darksome wood
A spacious grotto, all around o'er-grown
With hoary moss, and arch'd with pumice-stone.
From out its rocky clefts the waters flow,
And trickling swell into a lake below.
Nature had ev'ry where so plaid her part,
That ev'ry where she seem'd to vie with art.
Here the bright Goddess, toil'd and chaf'd with heat,
Was wont to bathe her in the cool retreat.

Here did she now with all her train resort,
Panting with heat, and breathless from the sport;
Her armour-bearer laid her bow aside,
Some loos'd her sandals, some her veil unty'd;
Each busy nymph her proper part undrest;
While Crocale, more handy than the rest,
Gather'd her flowing hair, and in a noose
Bound it together, whilst her own hung loose.
Five of the more ignoble sort by turns
Fetch up the water, and unlade the urns.

Now all undrest the shining Goddess stood,
When young Actaeon, wilder'd in the wood,
To the cool grott by his hard fate betray'd,
The fountains fill'd with naked nymphs survey'd.
The frighted virgins shriek'd at the surprize
(The forest echo'd with their piercing cries).
Then in a huddle round their Goddess prest:
She, proudly eminent above the rest,
With blushes glow'd; such blushes as adorn
The ruddy welkin, or the purple morn;
And tho' the crowding nymphs her body hide,

Half backward shrunk, and view'd him from a side.
Surpriz'd, at first she would have snatch'd her bow
But sees the circling waters round her flow;
These in the hollow of her hand she took,
And dash't 'em in his face, while thus she spoke:
'Tell, if thou can'st, the wond'rous sight disclos'd,
A Goddess naked to thy view expos'd.'

ADDISON

For the poet the words of the goddess are all important. Golding does even better, matching the rhythm to that of her repeated splashing:

'Now make the vaunt among thy mates, thou saw'st Diana bare.
Tell if thou can; I give thee leave. Tell hardly; do not spare.'

But Titian chooses to represent the terrible moment of silence that precedes this speech – a silence that is punctuated by the noisy confrontation between Diana's yapping lapdog and Actaeon's hound, his equivalent to the screeching nymphs. Earlier artists had painted the goddess splashing, yet this action, when depicted, seems incompatible with queenly dignity or tragic consequences. Diana's first reaction is to snatch her bow and Golding relates the look she 'casts' to an arrow she might have used (as in the expression 'if looks could kill') which Titian also represents:

And, casting back an angry look, like as she would have sent
An arrow at him had she had her bow there ready bent

GOLDING

Titian also gains a dramatic point by compressing the action that Ovid describes as a sequence. Thus one of the nymphs engaged in assisting the goddess has not yet seen what has happened – a device akin to that of the musicians continuing to play dance music after the hero has been assassinated in the last act of Giuseppe Verdi's *Un ballo in maschera*.

As mentioned above, Titian's grotto is clearly man-made, with a groin vault above, the water contained within a basin adorned with elegant relief carvings, whereas Ovid's grotto is natural. But the more we study Ovid the more we realise how carefully Titian has also done so. The episode opens with blood, and Titian introduces into this scene a mass of red drapery which is not only subliminally bloody, but also makes the shade and the water seem cooler, and draws out the flush of shame, heat and fury in the flesh of the goddess and her nymphs. Skin colour, and the eloquence of its changes, was of the greatest importance to both poet and painter.

Where the water has splashed on Actaeon's brow, the antlers of a stag begin to sprout. Other artists had depicted this moment but Titian chose not do so, surely because the expression on a human face elicits more sympathy, but also because, when visualised, the idea can appear as comic rather than tragic. However, the trophy of a stag's skull mounted on a pier and the hides of slain deer hanging in the distance allude to Actaeon's fate. He panics, begins to flee, is surprised by how swiftly he is able to move, sees himself reflected in a stream, tries in vain to speak, cannot decide where to turn. Then he is found by his pack of hounds who attack him. As he is torn to pieces he hears his own companions calling out for him, urging him to join the kill.

Ovid interrupts this conclusion by listing the names of thirty-two of Actaeon's hounds, an excursus that is avoided by Addison who also names only one of Diana's nymphs, Crocale, in the passage given above, although Ovid includes four others. But Golding, writing for a less metropolitan – and probably more masculine – public, follows Ovid with relish:

Strong Killbuck, currish Savage, Spring and Hunter fresh of smell,
And Lightfoot, who to lead a chase did bear away the bell;
Fierce Woodman, hurt not long ago in hunting of a boar;
And Shepherd, wont to follow sheep …

The roll call suggests the familial status of these hounds and thus the horror of what they do.

In his depiction of the *Death of Actaeon* Titian departs from Ovid by including Diana actually in pursuit of Actaeon, but in other respects he attends closely to the text – more closely than is at first apparent because of the unfinished character of this painting, which he seems originally to have planned as a companion to the portrayal of Diana surprised by Actaeon. Thus we do not at first see Actaeon's companion huntsmen, but they can be detected in the distance, and it is hard to discern in the water, front right, the reflection that reminds us of his terrible moment of recognition, and connects this painting with the other two, in which water and reflections play so large a part:

Now the hills he had played on so happily
Toyed with the echoes of his death-noises.
His head and antlers reared from the heaving pile.

And swayed – like the signalling arm
Of somebody drowning in surf.
But his friends, who had followed the pack

To this unexpected kill,
Urged them to finish the work. Meanwhile they shouted
For Actaeon – over and over for Actaeon

Ted Hughes, in these lines, was surely thinking of Titian, who shows Actaeon as still upright and with human arms, whereas in Ovid he has been completely transformed. Surf must also be a metaphor suggested by the brushstrokes of the painter. As a consequence of the public appeal to acquire it for the National

Gallery in 1972, Titian's painting had become one of the best-known works of art in Britain.

As for Titian's decision to include Diana herself, this may have been prompted by a desire to make the painting a better companion for Diana surprised by Actaeon – but with Diana now the hunter striding forward on the left. Perhaps he also intended to paint a set of four canvases and to match the *Death of Actaeon* with the fateful encounter of Callisto and Arcas. Had he painted this latter subject, he would have made the young male huntsman Arcas prominent and that perhaps explains why, in the *Death of Actaeon*, he portrays Diana presiding over the event, the most notable of his departures from Ovid.

Balance, contrast, interval, reversal and repetition are concerns common to both painters and poets. Titian's deliberate compositional instability – most obvious in his avoidance of verticals and horizontals even in a quasi-architectural setting – is as remarkable as the echoes of one painting in another. Never entirely satisfied, we are compelled to continue exploring the disturbing beauty of these paintings.

NICHOLAS PENNY

OVID'S METAMORPHOSES AND SELECTED TRANSLATIONS

LATIN

Ovid, *Metamorphoses*, Frank Justus Millar (trans.) revised by G.P. Goold, 2 vols, Cambridge, Mass.: Loeb Classical Library, 1916

ITALIAN

Ludovico Dolce, *Le Trasformationi*, Venice: G. Giolito de Ferrari, 1553

Giovanni Andrea dell'Anguillara, *De le Metamorfosi di Ovidio libri III*, Paris: A. Wechels, 1554

ENGLISH

Arthur Golding, *The Fyrst Fower Bookes of P. Ouidius Nasos worke, intitled Metamorphosis, translated oute of Latin into Englishe meter*, 4 pt, London: Willyam Seres, 1565
[There is a Penguin edition, published in 2002, and another published in 2008 by the Folio Society, illustrated with Titian's paintings.]

George Sandys, *Ovid's Metamorphosis Englished, Mythologiz'd, and Represented in Figures*, Oxford: John Lichfield, 1632

Samuel Garth, *Ovid's Metamorphoses in Fifteen Books. Translated [into English verse] by the most eminent hands* [viz., J. Dryden, J. Addison, L. Eusden, A. Mainwaring, S. Croxall, N. Tate, J. Gay, W. Congreve, and the editor Sir S. Garth, etc.], London: J. Tonson, 1717

Mary M. Innes, *The Metamorphoses of Ovid*, Harmondsworth: Penguin, 1955 (and frequently since)
[This is the best prose translation in modern English.]

A.D. Melville, *Ovid: Metamorphoses*, Oxford: Oxford University Press, 1986 (paperback 1987)

Ted Hughes, *Tales from Ovid: Twenty-Four Passages from the 'Metamorphoses'*, London: Faber, 1997

Titian (active about 1506; died 1576)
Diana and Actaeon, 1556–9
Oil on canvas, 184.5 x 202.2 cm
Bought jointly by the National Gallery and National Galleries of Scotland with contributions from the Scottish Government, the National Heritage Memorial Fund, The Monument Trust, The Art Fund (with a contribution from the Wolfson Foundation) and through public appeal, 2009, NG 6611

Titian (active about 1506; died 1576)
The Death of Actaeon, 1565–76
Oil on canvas, 178.4 x 198.1 cm
The National Gallery, London, NG 6420
Bought with a government grant and
contributions from The Art Fund, The Pilgrim
Trust and through public appeal, 1972

Titian (active about 1506; died 1576)
Diana and Callisto, 1556–9
Oil on canvas, 187 x 204.5 cm
Bought jointly by the National Gallery and National Galleries of Scotland with contributions from the National Lottery through the Heritage Lottery Fund, The Art Fund, The Monument Trust and through private appeal and bequests, 2012, NG 6616

ABOUT FACE

after Titian

Actaeon, you'll pay the price for looking
like a god; athletic, proud, immortal.
Diana, goddess of the hunt, will hound you.
She is too harsh; you should have looked at me.
I am her shadow, black yet fairer than
the mistress, clad in cloth finer than cirrus.
I want you, Actaeon. I wish I were
shroud white; O that you'd notice *me* and mouth
each monumental curve. Her handsome face
off-guard, you brushed aside the drape to see
how cool she bathed; with the pool's spray, she cursed you
for looking. In this pine-sweet grove, you turned
from man to horned and dappled stag: sentenced.
Look how your fate reflects itself in water.

Look! How your fate reflects itself in water
from man to horned and dappled stag, sentenced
for looking. In this pine-sweet grove, you turned.
How cool she bathed! With the pool's spray she cursed you.
Off-guard, you brushed aside the drape to see
each monumental curve, her handsome face
shroud white. O that you'd notice me and mouth
I want you. Actaeon, I wish I were
the mistress clad in cloth finer than cirrus.
I am her shadow, black yet fairer than
she is. Too harsh! You should have looked at me.
Diana, goddess of the hunt, will hound you
like a god, athletic, proud, immortal.
Actaeon, you'll pay the price for looking.

PATIENCE AGBABI

DIANA AND ACTAEON

The whole hillside being smeared and daubed
with the blood of the hunt, I dropped down
to a stream whose water ran clear and cool,
and followed its thread through a wooded fold,
among branches dressed with pelts and skulls.
Then stumbled headlong into that sacred grove.

That's when the universe pitched and groaned,
and I shrank from cloud-coloured flesh,
from calf and hip, curve and cleft,
from a writhing feast of fruit and meat:
salmon, silverside, redcurrant, peach;
from fingers worming for gowns and robes,
from eel and oyster, ankle and lip,
from bulb, bud, honeycomb, nest... And flinched

from Diana's arm bent back like a bow,
and flinched from Diana's naked glare –
a death-stare arrowed from eye to eye.
All seen in a blink but burnt on the mind.

The pink-red curtain of noon, drawn back,
unleashes the white wolves of the moon.

SIMON ARMITAGE

ACTAEON'S LOVER

I am the one half hidden by a pillar,
Gazing out at him with loving eyes,
Alarmed, although I cannot see his killer
Reacting to the terrible surprise.
A man! My secret love, who loved me too.
He used to meet me by a certain tree.
That day I couldn't make our rendezvous
Because the goddess said she needed me.
He searched the woods and stumbled on this place.
You know the rest: the dreadful way he died.
This moment: the last time I saw his face
Before the horror of the horns, the hide.
I rage and mourn. There can be no redress
Against divine Diana, murderess.

WENDY COPE

TITIAN: DIANA AND CALLISTO

Girls, look where I point:
it's not about her belly's soft pout,
or a god whose name is a planet,
whether she was or wasn't compliant
when she heard him pant
as his seed was spent,
each bruise on her skin his fingerprint,
her unfit to bathe in so much as a pint
of our sacred stream, pregnant, penitent;
not about any of that, even should she repent
or prove her innocence conclusively, pin it
on him, on the stars, on myth, plant
the thought that she's the victim here; my point,
ladies, is this – it's all about paint.

CAROL ANN DUFFY

THE DARK

What was I in their story? The dark.
An electric unknown, a girl
who slipped off the path and found
herself alone in the forest's locked room,
who set aside her quiver and bow
and lay down. When I woke
the world was in bright version.
I believed what I saw. He was not
what I saw. My body opened.
It was not my body. I became
a question that must not be asked
of the gods. I grew ripe with it.
I lost my place, my people.
I took the white ribbon from my hair.
Yet to her I was still what lit him.
She reached down and obscured my form.
My voice at first gaudy with argument
took on a rip, wrench and boom.
My body warped and cracked.
I was sinew and claw, my odour
that of a crowded cave in winter.
I was night torn from day.
I ran to escape my own shadow.
The beasts of the forest drove me out.
The villagers barred their doors.
The gods turned the page.

LAVINIA GREENLAW

DIANA AND ACTAEON

And you, sir, yes, sir, you who just began
to read these lines you're, maybe, a marked man.
Haven't you half thought that while you view
Actaeon's intrusion you're intruding too?
Perhaps too chubby for most modern tastes
for less ample pulchritude and skinny waists,
Diana, scorned by connoisseurs of scrawn,
punishes those who'd pimp her as plump porn.

Actaeon stares at the stag skull, the flayed skin
above the nymph who dries Diana's shin.
The stag skull in its dominant position
over mortal flesh immortalised by Titian,
maybe marks you out to share Actaeon's doom
after you've left the safety of this room.

On those Diana's flesh makes salivate
and clock the stag skull's sockets far too late
stiff sprouting hairs will suddenly appear
and flesh-hooked faces fur up like doomed deer.

As you exit through the gallery's glass doors
that antlered head reflected, is it yours?
For survival's sake when leaving best beware
of baying bloodhounds in Trafalgar Square.

TONY HARRISON

ACTAEON

High burdened brow, the antlers that astound,
Arms that end now in two hardened feet,
His nifty haunches, pointed ears and fleet
Four-legged run... In the pool he saw a crowned
Stag's head and heard something that groaned
When he tried to speak. And it was no human sweat
That steamed off him: he was like a beast in heat,
As if he'd prowled and stalked until he found

The grove, the grotto and the bathing place
Of the goddess and her nymphs, as if he'd sought
That virgin nook deliberately, as if
His desires were hounds that had quickened pace
On Diana's scent before his own pack wrought
Her vengeance on him, at bay beneath the leaf-

lit woodland. There his branchy antlers caught
When he faced the hounds
That couldn't know him as they bayed and fought
And tore out mouthfuls of hide and flesh and blood
From what he was, while his companions stood
Impatient for the kill, assessing wounds.

SEAMUS HEANEY

WOODLAND BURIAL

Thrown water touched him and where it touched it said
his body was the same brownness leaves turn
when autumn is upon us, a swept-up heap
trembling where it stood,
that when the huntress concentrated
trees, tree-shadows, underbrush and bushes made a wood
and it was ever thus, that nothing can be other than as known
by a god, no truth a lie, no death long sleep.

Poised with springy longbow drawn
and back to the sun, the one who had revealed her form
from landscape or eyes
independent as a streak of white paint on a mirror
held him on her gaze
and held the torn canopy of clouds on the water
how she might have kept a spoonful of honey in the warm
fold of her tongue before it dissipated.

Not the greatest possible harm,
which needs to be known and named as such
to achieve its end, not what he fled, but the unofficial crime,
the moment she let her attention crop
those deep recursive avenues of beech to a backdrop
he broke against, confused,
so nothing in the landscape escaped his touch
and nothing left of him was in the picture she composed.

FRANCES LEVISTON

DIANA AND ACTAEON

It could be over Strangford Lough:
that hoop of sky beyond the archway
with its midsummer blue of a northern country
and corridor of clouds

and Actaeon the servant
standing slack-jawed in the doorway
having stupidly dropped the chocolate tray—
a whole life's wages' worth of china

exploding in confetti
no praying to all the Saints in Heaven
might possibly take back, lift up, undo,
obliterate—

like the sight of his reverend mistress
caught languidly *in flagrante*
with five of the shyest housemaids
and a cousin from the city.

Stone animals crouched in the dusky gardens
cover their ears. And immediately
he sees, in the uplifted anvil
of her naked heel, his punishment—

whipping, stocking, damaged hands,
a four-day journey south, or, if he's lucky,
a sign slung round his neck
—*houseboy for hire*—

out in Van Diemen's Land.

SINÉAD MORRISSEY

A CALL

vellet abesse quidem, sed adest
Ovid, *Metamorphoses*, III

A winter train. A gale, a poacher's moon.
The black glass. Do I honestly still blame
the wrong turn in the changing rooms I took
when I was six, and stood too long to look?
The scream Miss Venner loosed at me. 'The *nerve*!'
I was ablaze. And it was worth the shame,
I thought; of course I did. It was too soon
to tell the dream from what I'd paid for it.
Then soon too late. Two sides of the same door.
So was it the recoil or the release
that lashed the world so out of shape? Tonight
I stare right through the face that I deserve
as all my ghost dogs gather at the shore,
behind them the whole sea like the police.

DON PATERSON

THE CHANGE

The goddess with her killer glare:
no problem there. I've seen that look myself
often enough, aimed straight at me,
and it wasn't hard to swivel it
through ninety degrees and fix it in profile.
(That dinky quiver, wrong size for the bow,
I'll adjust later.) The dogs, too, I can handle,
if I can keep the brushwork fluent:
less a pack of them than a flood, a torrent,
of muscular flanks and backs and squabbling
yelps and scent-maddened muzzles
dragging your man down. Now, he's the trouble,
which is why I've put him in the middle distance,
an arrow's flight away. He's turning into a stag.
But how do you do that, exactly?
Head first, as I've tried here, following Ovid?
Ping! – he's got antlers and a long neck,
but the rest of his body's slow on the uptake,
so he's left looking less like prey brought low
than some tipsy idiot taking a spill at a carnival?
Forget it. What I want is the change itself,
when he's neither man nor beast, or somehow both at once,
and you don't just see but feel the combined
horror and justice of his fate. Some way to go.
Never mind, I'll be patient. It can wait.

CHRISTOPHER REID

CALLISTO'S SONG

* stars * stars * stars * stars * and * I *
 * am * made * of * them * now * looking *
* down * on * myself * then * a * colorito * woman * yes *
 * that * was * me * in * my * red * sandals * the * great *
* outdoors * curtained * golden * embroidered *
 * and * heatshimmer * above * blue * mountains *
* nothing * vertical * not * even * the * plinth* and *
 * no * speech * no * names * then * just * a * cry *
* as * the * busy * body * nymphs * stripped * me * because *
 * we * all * had * rounded * bellies * then * but *
* nine * months * gone * so * my * navel * curved *
 * like * a * gash * and * o * so * noticeable *
* among * all * the * diagonals * and * everyone *
 * looking * a * different * way * looking * a * lot *
* especially * the * goddess * at * me * her * arrow-arm *
 * pointing * bow-mouth * strung * and * dogs * crouched *
* because * they * sensed * consequences * and * gods *
 * arriving * and * doing * what * gods * do * upstairs * and *
* the * artist's * finger * loaded * and * the * paint * alive *
 * alive * with * stars * stars * stars * stars * stars *

JO SHAPCOTT

ACTAEON

O, my America, my Newfoundland
John Donne, Elegy 20

O, my America, discovered by slim chance,
behind, as it seemed, a washing line
I shoved aside without thinking –
does desire have thoughts or define
its object, consuming all in a glance?

You, with your several flesh sinking
upon itself in attitudes of hurt,
while the dogs at my heels
growl at the strange red shirt
under a horned moon, you, drinking

night water – tell me what the eye steals
or borrows. What can't we let go
without protest? My own body turns
against me as I sense it grow
contrary. Whatever night reveals

is dangerously toothed. And so the body burns
as if torn by sheer profusion of skin
and cry. It wears its ragged dress
like something it once found comfort in,
the kind of comfort even a dog learns

by scent. So flesh falls away, ever less
human, like desire itself, though pain
still registers in the terrible balance
the mind seems so reluctant to retain,
o, my America, my nakedness!

GEORGE SZIRTES

ACTAEON

I thought of all my girlfriends
gathered together on a stage,
each of them holding up her year
and smiling attractively.
I lifted one corner of the curtain
and there they all were,
but shy and resentful now,
covering themselves from my sight.

'I didn't know you girls all
knew one another,' I said,
seeing only a tumble of looks and limbs.
'What are you doing here?'
They answered that they might as well
ask me the same question.
What was the matter?
Couldn't I make up my mind?

If I had stood my ground
and said nothing, or claimed
to be just passing through,
I might have escaped their mockery,
I might have been forgiven.
Alas, I fled the scene,
dogged by indecision and regret,
torn apart by my imaginings.

HUGO WILLIAMS

ACKNOWLEDGEMENT
Extracts from 'Actaeon' taken from *Tales from Ovid* © 2012 Estate of Ted Hughes and reprinted by permission of Faber and Faber Ltd.